THE
Crayola
OPPOSITES
BOOK

JODIE SHEPHERD

LERNER PUBLICATIONS ◆ MINNEAPOLIS

TO ALL MY READERS: ALWAYS BE THE OPPOSITE OF UNINTERESTED—BE CURIOUS!

Official Licensed Product
Lerner Publications Company
A division of Lerner Publishing Group, Inc.
241 First Avenue North
Minneapolis, MN 55401 USA

For reading levels and more information, look up this title at www.lernerbooks.com.

Main body text set in Billy Infant Regular 24/30.
Typeface provided by SparkyType.

Library of Congress Cataloging-in-Publication Data

Names: Shepherd, Jodie, author.
Title: The Crayola opposites book / by Jodie Shepherd.
Description: Minneapolis : Lerner Publications, 2017. | Series: Crayola concepts | Includes
    bibliographical references and index. | Audience: Ages 4-9. | Audience: K to Grade 3.
Identifiers: LCCN 2016050977 (print) | LCCN 2016052678 (ebook) | ISBN 9781512432879 (lb :
    alk. paper) | ISBN 9781512455694 (pb : alk. paper) | ISBN 9781512449259 (eb pdf)
Subjects: LCSH: English language—Synonyms and antonyms—Juvenile literature. | CYAC:
    English language—Synonyms and antonyms—Pictorial works.
Classification: LCC PE1591 .S448 2017 (print) | LCC PE1591 (ebook) | DDC 428.1—dc23

LC record available at https://lccn.loc.gov/2016050977

Manufactured in the United States of America
1-41818-23778-3/13/2017

Table of Contents

WHAT ARE OPPOSITES?

Opposites are completely different. They come in pairs, like big and small.

OPPOSITE PAIRS

Short and tall are opposites.

What opposites can you find in nature?

Textures can be opposites.

A toad is bumpy.

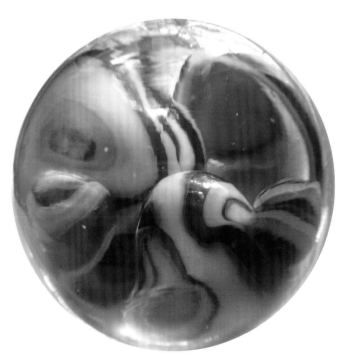

A marble is smooth.

To make something in your picture look bumpy, try drawing lots of tiny dots close together. This is called stippling.

The red pail is full of sand.

The yellow pail is empty.

What other opposites can you find at the beach?

Hot and cold are opposites. Cocoa is hot and steamy. Lemonade is cold and icy.

Did you know colors can be warm and cool? Red, orange, and yellow are called warm colors. Blue, green, and purple are called cool colors.

TWO IN ONE!

Dark and light are opposites.

Part of this sand dune is in sunshine.

Another part is in shadow.

A roller coaster goes up and down.

It also goes slow and fast. *Wheee!*

Piano keys can be black or white—

a dark shade and a light one.

Can you draw a picture using only black and white?

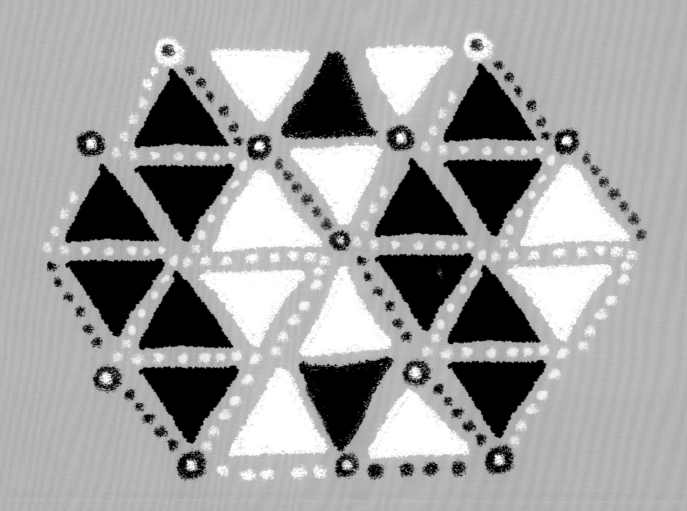

THE END AND THE BEGINNING

You open a book to read it. You close it at the end!

There are many other opposites in the world. What kinds do you see every day? How many pairs can you come up with?

WORLD OF COLORS

Even some colors are opposites! Here are some of the Crayola® crayon colors used in this book. Can you find them in the photos?

WILD STRAWBERRY

MANGO TANGO

BANANA MANIA

SCREAMIN' GREEN

JUNGLE GREEN

PERIWINKLE

MIDNIGHT BLUE

BLACK

GLOSSARY

opposite: a person, thing, or idea that is completely different from another

pair: a set of two objects

sand dune: a hill of sand piled up by the wind

shade: a slightly lighter or darker color than the original color

shadow: darker areas created when light is blocked

steamy: hot and humid (as in water evaporating into steam)

stippling: adding tiny dots of color or texture

texture: the feel or look of a surface that's not flat

TO LEARN MORE

BOOKS

Brooks, Erik. *Polar Opposites*. Tarrytown, NY: Marshall Cavendish Children, 2010. Read this fun story about a polar bear and a penguin that are very opposite but still best friends!

Seeger, Laura Vaccaro. *Black? White! Day? Night! A Book of Opposites*. New York: Roaring Brook, 2016. Lift the flaps in this fun book to discover the opposite of the picture on the page.

Wilson, Karma. *Big Bear, Small Mouse*. New York: Margaret K. McElderry Books, 2016. Read more about opposites in this story about big Bear and small Mouse.

WEBSITES

"A Game of Opposites"
http://www.meddybemps.com/opposites/Index.html
Test which opposites you know with this online game. How many opposites can you name?

Lion & Lamb
http://www.crayola.com/crafts/lion--lamb-craft/
Create art with opposites! Paint a lion and a lamb in this project. What other animals could be called opposites?

INDEX

PHOTO ACKNOWLEDGMENTS

The images in this book are used with the permission of: Mark_KA/Shutterstock.com, p. 5 (top left); Marcos Mesa Sam Wordley/Shutterstock.com, p. 5 (top right); tratong/Shutterstock.com, p. 5 (bottom left); © Jennifer Russell/Dreamstime.com, p. 5 (bottom right); © iStockphoto.com/GlobalP, p. 5 (center); © iStockphoto.com/best-photo, p. 6; © iStockphoto.com/SundariJi, p. 7; © Sikth/Dreamstime.com, p. 8 (left); © Myrthe Krook/Dreamstime.com, p. 8 (right); © Matthew Benoit/Dreamstime.com, p. 10 (left); © Petr Malyshev/Dreamstime.com, p. 10 (right); © iStockphoto.com/Csondy, p. 11; © Pixelrobot/Dreamstime.com, p. 12 (left); © Edith Layland/Dreamstime.com, p. 12 (right); JaySi/Shutterstock.com, pp. 14-15; © iStockphoto.com/smaehl, p. 16; © iStockphoto.com/Watcha, p. 18; © iStockphoto.com/tanuha2001, p. 20; © Burazin/Photographer's Choice/Getty Images, p. 21 (top left); © joSon/The Image Bank/Getty Images, p. 21 (top right); Joe Doylem/Alamy Stock Photo, p. 21 (bottom left); © iStockphoto.com/Balefire9, p. 21 (bottom right); © iStockphoto.com/Flutter_97321, p. 21 (center).

Cover: © iStockphoto.com/bozzybozza (drinks); © iStockphoto.com/Watcha (piano keys); © Royalty-Free/CORBIS (elephants).

LERNER
e SOURCE

Expand learning beyond the printed book. Download free, complementary educational resources for this book from our website, www.lerneresource.com.